THE WRIGHT WORKBOOK
For A Victorious Life

ANTONIO VAN'KEITH WRIGHT

THE WRIGHT WORKBOOK

Copyright © 2025 by Antonio V. Wright

All rights reserved. No part of this publication may be reproduced, distributed, or transmitted in any form or by any means, including photocopying, recording, or other electronic or mechanical methods, without the prior written permission of the publisher, except in the case of brief quotations embodied in critical reviews and certain other noncommercial uses permitted by copyright law. For permission requests, email the publisher:

Attention: Permissions Coordinator

Welcome To The Storm Publishing!
info@midnightstorm.net

Ordering Information:
Quantity sales. Special discounts are available on quantity purchases by corporations, associations, and others. For details, contact the publisher at the email address above.

Orders by U.S. trade bookstores and wholesalers.

Library of Congress Control Number: 978-1-966612-52-0

ISBN: 978-1-966612-46-9

Cover Design: Beenish Khan

Veronica Miller, Red Diamond Editing by V. Rena,

reddiamondediting5@yahoo.com

First Printed Edition: August 2025

Printed in the United States of America

Table of Contents

CHAPTER 1 1
    PLAN 1
Chapter 2 4
    Purpose 4
Chapter 3 7
    Preparation 7
Chapter 4 10
    Choices 10
Chapter 5 13
    Friends 13
Chapter 6 16
    Leadership 16
Chapter 7 19
    Discipline 19
Chapter 8 22
    Thank You 22
Chapter 9 25
    Perseverance 25
Chapter 10 28
    Perspective 28
Chapter 11 31

Responsibility	31
Chapter 12	**34**
Conflict	34
Chapter 13	**37**
Critical Thinking	37
Chapter 14	**41**
Prayer	41
Chapter 15	**44**
Vision	44
Chapter 16	**47**
Determination	47
Chapter 17	**50**
Reliability	50
Chapter 18	**53**
Forgive	53
Chapter 19	**56**
Relentless	56
Chapter 20	**59**
Resilient	59
About the Author	**63**

ANTONIO VAN'KEITH WRIGHT

ACKNOWLEDGEMENTS

I have an enormous number of influencers who helped me learn the skills to develop this workbook. Some showed me in my early years the man I did not want to be. Others showed me how to trust God, work hard, and sacrifice by giving my time and money. My mother taught me a lot about life, but she could not teach me how to be a man. I am *a man* in every sense of the word today because of men like Coach Stanley Blackmon and my pastor/stepfather, Apostle William Cooper. I want to also acknowledge some men who have been taken from us but who will never be forgotten. These men were some of the best fathers I ever met: Anselyum Odell Lee, Sr., Willie Harvey, Jr., Johnny Miller, and Jacob Rush, Sr.

FOREWORD

Latrenda Chirell Bailey-Rush, Ed.S.

The Wright Workbook for a Victorious Life has been an inspiration. Being a part this project has been beyond a blessing. Mr. Antonio Wright has poured his all into laying the foundation for those who are looking to better themselves and grow deep into what they were designed to do on this earth. Living on purpose is the goal. Everyone has a purpose, and being *intentional* about every detail of your life has to be top priority. Antonio not only shares his life experience but also illustrates how he learned to keep going despite the letdowns that he has encountered throughout his life. So, as you read this word from such an annointed man of God, allow each chapter to resonate within and begin to examine how you can begin to make the necessary changes needed to improve your life. I can guarantee that having *The Wright Workbook for a Victorious Life* as your guide will help you have a victorious life.

ANTONIO VAN'KEITH WRIGHT

My TESTIMONY

Can you imagine being the biggest, strongest guy in your school?

Everybody loves you and they think that you're cool!

However, I believe my Father in heaven is saying, "My son is acting like a fool."

While being a college football star, I knew nothing about being humble, did not realize,

Until February 2nd of 1997 when a car accident left me paralyzed.

I was thrown from my Pathfinder 100 feet in the sky.

I was stuck on the side of the highway, in the spot where I was supposed to die.

I was confused and I didn't know why.

I was left on this earth, forced to use this wheelchair.

The body I knew was gone, as well as my NFL career.

My life felt out of control. My hopes were spilled.

Until a month later on March 2nd my baby brother was killed.

Now Christ had given me a cross I wish I did not have to bear.

THE WRIGHT WORKBOOK

What was I going to do? Give up and quit because life was hard and unfair?

Not me. I refused to quit because I was fully aware.

Someone needed to see me bear this cross in my wheelchair.

Now I have committed myself to the one and only Christ.

I have accepted my purpose to live a life of sacrifice.

CHAPTER 1
PLAN

When I was in school, we were taught how to write an essay. The first thing the teachers taught us to do back then was to create an outline. To be efficient and successful, you need to map out your thoughts, find a title, an introductory paragraph, and follow the steps to complete the plan. Why is this part so important? It teaches us to develop *a plan* before we started implementing the process. See, there are steps to success.

What I hope to do in this book is to give you a *strategic plan* to achieve a victorious future. However, this book can only give you tools to put in your tool bag. To soar, you must use the tools you receive and make the right choices. The responsibility doesn't lie in how many tools you've collected but in what you do with them. You can have everything you need to succeed, but if you never take the time to apply the knowledge, your toolbox becomes nothing more than storage. Victory requires *movement*, it requires *intention*, and it demands *the will* to keep pressing forward even when the journey gets hard.

In the National Football League's long history, there has only been one team that went undefeated for a whole season, the Miami Dolphins in 1972. That means every NFL champion except one has faced at least one defeat. Victory does not mean you never lose. It means that despite the setback or the challenge, you choose to keep moving forward anyway. You get up, brush yourself off, and step into the next moment with focus, discipline, and hope. That's what separates those who only dream of success from those who are willing to work for it and walk in it fully.

The gift of victory does not come by accident. You do not just walk down the street and suddenly, victory falls into your lap. Start with a *defined goal*. Prepare a sequence of steps to reach that goal. It takes a plan. And it takes your decision to follow that plan even when it gets tough, even when others around you quit, and even when you feel like throwing in the towel yourself.

Victory is not for the perfect. It is for **the persistent**. You may fall. You may fail. You may have moments of doubt and delay. But if you choose to rise each time, you come back stronger, wiser, and more focused than before. This book is not magic, but it can be a mirror. A mirror to show you your strength, your options, and your strategy. If you are ready to put one foot in front of the other, then turn the page and let's begin mapping your victory, one step, one choice, and one goal at a time.

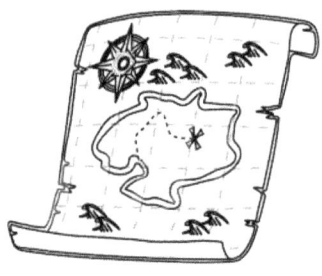

What is your top goal for this year?

_____
_____
_____

What steps will you take to reach your goal?

_____
_____
_____
_____
_____
_____
_____
_____
_____

Chapter 2

Purpose

As a young Black man growing up in the late 1980s and early 1990s in urban Jackson, Mississippi, I was delusional—until I came to understand that everything in life was created for a purpose. Anything ever made, designed, manufactured, or mass produced was done so with a specific reason in mind. A product may be used in all kinds of ways, but it was originally designed to do one particular job.

For example, Air Jordan tennis shoes were created to wear on your feet. They were made for comfort, performance, and style on the basketball court and in everyday life. But someone could put dirt in them and use them to grow flowers. And while that might be creative, it completely ignores the original purpose for which they were made. That was not why they were created.

I remember when my wife used to bring furniture home for me to put together. Whether it was a desk or a table, it always came in a box with a picture on the front. Confident and stubborn, I opened the box, dumped out all the parts, and immediately started putting it together without ever reading the instructions. I always thought I could figure it out just by looking at the picture, as if I knew what the creator had in mind. But time after time, I ended up with extra parts, lopsided legs, and furniture that didn't stand up straight.

Eventually, my wife got tired of watching me fail. She stopped bringing home furniture for me to assemble and decided it was better to let the creator put it together and ship it to us. At least then, she could trust that it would stand firm, be balanced, and serve its intended purpose.

That lesson stuck with me. In many ways, it's the same with life. **We all were created on purpose, for a purpose**. But when we ignore our instructions—when we refuse to listen to the Creator—it becomes easy to get off balance, misuse our gifts, or forget our value. We end up trying to function based on assumptions instead of *divine* design.

You do not want to be like a pair of Air Jordans used to grow flowers. Sure, something might still grow, but that was never the reason they were made. In the same way, you don't want to spend your life being useful in the wrong way. You were not designed to just exist, to just get by, or to settle for less than your purpose.

Purpose gives you direction. It gives you peace. And most of all, it reminds you that your existence is *intentional*. You are not a mistake, an afterthought, or an accident. You were formed with precision, with gifts no one else has, and with an assignment only you can fulfill.

So, before you keep building your life based on what you think the picture on the outside of the box looks like, pause. Read the instructions. Connect with the Creator. Because the one who designed you knows what you were created to become. And when you walk in that truth, there are no extra parts, no missing pieces—just purpose, perfectly assembled.

What is your purpose in life? Why are you here?

_____
_____
_____
_____
_____
_____
_____
_____
_____
_____

Chapter 3
Preparation

The definition of *preparation* is the state of making something ready for use. My old coach used to say, "Prior planning prevents poor performance." Back then, I thought he was just stringing together a bunch of "P" words to sound important. I didn't realize he was planting seeds of wisdom that would one day shape my future. Now that I've gone through life—experiencing both losses and opportunities—I've come to understand just how right he was. Preparation makes all the difference. If I am already ready, then I don't have to get ready.

I learned something about myself and my study habits a long time ago. I was not like other children. While some kids could study for two nights and make an A plus, I needed three solid weeks just to earn that A minus. At first, this frustrated me. But then I realized it was teaching me something greater—discipline, time management, and the power of intentional effort. I couldn't afford to procrastinate. I had to get my work done immediately. See, I learned that if you are always early, you are always on time. And if you're always on time, you're never caught off guard.

Growing up, whenever I asked my mother how to spell a word, she would say, "Go look it up." At the time, that response irritated me. We had three thick dictionaries in the house, and I never understood how I was supposed to look up a word if I didn't already know how to spell it. But that challenge forced me to think, to guess, and to try. It taught me to work through problems, not wait for easy answers. That kind of resourcefulness stuck with me.

Today, things are different. Every young person has a phone and access to Google. The tools for learning are literally in your hands. There is no reason—none at all—why someone should not do their research to find out what, where, why, how, and who as it relates to anything they are trying to accomplish. Preparation is not a luxury; it's *a necessity*. We live in a world where access to information is everywhere, and yet, *effort* still makes the difference.

Prior planning prevents poor performance. If you are ready, then you don't have to get ready. If you are always early, you are always on time.

These aren't just catchy sayings. They are principles that have been tested and proven in my life. Preparation opens doors. It builds confidence. It allows you to walk into a room, an interview, an opportunity—not hoping you belong, but knowing you're equipped.

Therefore, I challenge you to take these nuggets of wisdom and apply them to your life. Let preparation become a habit. Let discipline become your routine. Don't just wish for success, plan for it. And when your moment comes, you'll be ready not just to show up, but to shine.

How can you do a better job preparing for a big assignment or project?

_____
_____
_____
_____
_____
_____
_____
_____
_____
_____
_____

Chapter 4
Choices

We are the sum of the *choices* we make. Every decision—big or small—adds up over time and shapes the direction of our lives. When I was young, I was a member of a gang. I won't sit here and pretend that I made all good choices. The truth is, I made a lot of bad ones. But I also learned something powerful: it wasn't just the things I said "yes" to that mattered. It was the things I chose to say "no" to that helped shape the man I am today.

There came a time when I had to start saying "no" to things that were easy, but dangerous. I had to say "no" to shortcuts, "no" to peer pressure, and "no" to people who didn't want to see me win. Saying "no" became just as important as saying "yes"—because every "no" I gave to destruction created space for a "yes" to growth, peace, and purpose.

If you make a lot of good choices, that will equal a life filled with fulfilled promises, a life of direction, stability, and completed goals. Good choices don't always feel exciting in the moment, but over time, they build a foundation that's unshakable. If you choose to volunteer, work overtime, give extra effort on assignments, submit your work on time or early, do your chores without being reminded, and take responsibility by completing tasks around the house, you will reap many rewards. These choices shape your character. They create discipline. And when practiced at a young age, they can lead to a successful life and position you to one day help someone else make better choices, too.

However, it's just as important to understand that there are real consequences to making bad choices. For example, if a person decides to go left, knowing deep down they should go right, they must be prepared to deal with whatever comes next. You cannot outrun consequences. They may not show up immediately, but they always arrive. And sometimes, the hardest part about consequences isn't the punishment—it's **the regret**. That feeling of knowing you could have chosen differently. That weight of wondering what could have been.

Regret can stay with you for a lifetime. But so can pride. When you make the right choice—even when it's hard—you walk away with peace. You walk away knowing you took the higher road. And the benefits that follow? They last a lifetime, too.

THE WRIGHT WORKBOOK

So remember, every choice you make becomes a brick in the path you're building. Choose wisely. Choose intentionally. Because while one wrong turn doesn't define your whole story, it can delay your destination. But with every right choice, you get closer to the life you were created to live.

What bad choices have you made in the past that you do not want to repeat?

_____
_____
_____
_____

What good choices do you want to continue to make?

_____
_____
_____
_____
_____

Chapter 5
Friends

My mother used to tell me, "**Birds of a feather flock together.**" Back then, I thought she just had a collection of old sayings that didn't mean much. But now, I understand exactly what she was trying to teach me. See, I have never seen an eagle and a pigeon fly together. I've never seen a crow and a hawk soaring side by side. And the reason is simple—they are different types of birds, built for different heights, different purposes, and different journeys.

One of the problems we face as people is that we start mimicking each other—often without even realizing it. I've noticed that if you spend enough time around someone, you'll start to pick up their habits. You'll begin dressing alike, speaking the same phrases, listening to the same music, and even thinking the same way. It's human nature to adapt to your environment. But the real question is not *if* you'll start mimicking your friends—the real question is *which* friends do you want to mimic?

Some people are content with staying grounded. They don't want to grow, take risks, or leave their comfort zone. Those are your pigeons. And that's okay—for them. But if you have a calling to fly higher, you need to recognize who's built for that kind of flight. I've learned to distinguish eagles from pigeons. I love everyone, and I treat all people with respect, but I only keep a few close friends who can truly fly with me. The ones who soar higher, dream bigger, and challenge me to be better.

There are a lot of people who know my name. Plenty of people have memories of good times we've shared, laughs we've had, and moments we enjoyed. But only a handful truly know my story. Only a few were there when I was broken, when I struggled, when I almost gave up. These friends have seen the good, the bad, and everything in between. They didn't just stick around for the party—they showed up during the storm. That's how I know they're eagles. They were made to fly high, and they don't get shaken by a little wind.

Not everyone is meant to go where you're going. Not everyone can handle the altitude. Some people were never meant to fly that high, and that's okay. But if you want to reach your full potential, you have to be careful who you surround yourself with. Because who you fly with matters. **Choose your friends wisely.**

ANTONIO VAN'KEITH WRIGHT

Which friends bring out the best in you?

_____
_____
_____
_____

Which friends get you in trouble?

_____
_____
_____
_____

Which friends will you choose to keep?

_____
_____
_____
_____
_____

Chapter 6

Leadership

People who watch you will observe the way you approach problems and how you either fail or succeed. That outcome will influence others to either want to follow your lead or follow someone else. They will be persuaded to either be like you or be nothing like you. Whether you realize it or not, your actions are shaping someone's opinion. That's why I honestly believe that how well a person *leads* is a choice.

If you are a reliable teammate, then you are already leading by example. When people can count on you to be consistent, respectful, honest, and committed, they begin to trust your leadership—whether you hold a title or not. You don't need to be the loudest or most popular person in the room to be a leader. You just need to be the one others can count on.

Mainly, you must show up. That alone makes a huge difference. We all have fears, and sometimes, those fears come true. Things don't go our way. We mess up. We fall short. But when we choose to keep going, when we do what's needed in spite of our fear, that is *leadership*. That is *strength*.

Be in school every day. That is leading by example. Even when you're tired. Even when things at home are rough. Even when you feel like giving up. Your presence speaks volumes. Even if your failures start to add up, show up. Even when you haven't completed your assignment or prepared for the exam, show up. You're not showing up because you're perfect, you're showing up because you are *determined* to grow.

By showing up every day, you are visually telling your friends, your family, your classmates, and your teachers that you are willing to keep trying no matter what. You are saying, "I may not have it all together, but I care enough to be present. I care enough to try again." And that matters.

People are always watching you, whether they say it or not. Someone younger may be looking to you for motivation. A peer may be leaning on your consistency as their reminder to keep going. You never know who is being encouraged by your effort. Remember, others are watching you. **You are leading by example.**

THE WRIGHT WORKBOOK

Where are you leading your friends?

_____
_____
_____
_____
_____
_____
_____
_____
_____
_____
_____
_____
_____
_____
_____
_____
_____
_____
_____

Chapter 7
Discipline

I went to seven elementary schools in six years. So, all I ever wanted to do was fit in. Every time I started over at a new school, I felt like the outcast. I was always the new student, walking into classrooms where friendships had already been formed. A guy like me thought the cool kids were always found in the back few rows of the classroom. They laughed the loudest, talked the most, and never seemed worried about homework or grades. Naturally, I believed that if I sat with them, maybe I could belong, too.

But the only problem with that logic was this—whenever I was with the group that was making trouble, I got in trouble, too. It didn't matter if I didn't say much or if I was just trying to be part of the crowd. My presence alone got me lumped into the wrong group, and I started realizing that I was losing out—on trust, on opportunities, and most importantly, on progress.

That's when I learned something valuable. I made the decision to distinguish myself—not by being louder, not by trying to outdo anyone, but by being *disciplined* enough to sit on the first or second row in class. The kids who cracked jokes, threw paper, or talked back were never sitting up front. So, when I moved my seat, I ***moved my mindset.*** I couldn't be mistaken for one of them anymore, and for the first time, I had space to focus.

Most of all, I got to put my full concentration into completing my goal of getting better grades than I did the year before. You know that promise you make to yourself every summer? That silent vow that next year will be different. I made that promise before fifth grade, again before sixth, and again before seventh. But year after year, I didn't change my actions—I just hoped for a new outcome. And as you probably already know, hope without discipline is a setup for disappointment. If you don't commit to the discipline that's required, you will fail in your repeated attempts.

The personal decision to distinguish myself through discipline—to set myself apart from every other student, every athlete, and every young Black man who might've been doubted or dismissed—turned out to be one of the best decisions I ever made. That one change, that one choice to do things differently, followed me through middle school, carried me through high school, and shaped my entire future.

Discipline didn't just help me make honor roll. It helped me graduate with honors—from both high school and college. It helped me silence the noise and focus on what really mattered. And most importantly, it reminded me that I didn't have to blend in to be valuable. I just had to show up, work hard, and stay consistent.

The world may try to tell you where you belong, but discipline will show the world where you're going.

How can you distinguish yourself by being more disciplined?

_____
_____
_____
_____
_____
_____
_____
_____
_____
_____
_____
_____
_____

Chapter 8

Thank You

There is nothing more valuable—and nothing easier to give—than *praise*. The Bible says, *"Praise him for his mighty acts: praise him according to his excellent greatness."* —Psalms 150:2. That verse is a reminder that praise isn't just a response to something good happening—it's an expression of who God is and what He continues to do in our lives, whether we see it all clearly or not.

When I wake up each morning, the first thing I do is pray and thank God. I praise Him for another day of life, another opportunity to grow, to love, to heal, and to serve. I praise Him for my pain because even in the struggle, there's something He's shaping in me. I praise Him for everyone who loves me, and I even praise Him for those who may not have my best interests at heart—because they've taught me just as much as my supporters have.

Over the years, I've learned that a simple "Thank you" carries incredible weight. It may seem small, but it can make someone feel deeply appreciated—especially when that person has shown up for you, sacrificed for you, or helped you in your time of need. A sincere "Thank you" can calm anger, mend wounds, and strengthen relationships. It has *power*. And if we can recognize how much power there is in thanking people, then imagine the power that comes from consistently praising and thanking God.

Take a moment and really think about that. What if you gave persistent praise to God—not just when everything is going right, but when it's all going wrong? What if you learned to say "Thank you" in the middle of the storm? What if your praise didn't depend on your comfort but on your conviction?

Let me be clear: I don't want anyone to get confused. I don't care how bad it is. I don't care how much you're hurting. I don't care how uncomfortable life feels right now. You still have a reason to praise. Why? Because no matter how difficult your situation may seem, there is someone in this world who has it worse. And yet, there are people who have less than you, who still find a way to be grateful.

Gratitude is not about having everything you want—it's about recognizing the value of what you *do* have. You must learn to thank God for what you have and stop focusing on what you don't. The enemy would love for you to waste your days comparing, complaining, and feeling defeated. But praise silences all that noise. Praise reminds you that God is still good. That He still has a plan. That you are still breathing and therefore still have purpose.

So today, start with "Thank you." Thank Him for life, for lessons, for breath, and even for brokenness—because broken things in God's hands still have value.

Let your praise be persistent, not passive. Make it a daily habit. Make it a way of life.

Because there is always something to be thankful for.

Who can you say "Thank you" to today?

_____
_____
_____
_____
_____
_____
_____
_____
_____

Chapter 9

Perseverance

On February 2, 1992, I was in a motor vehicle accident that left me paralyzed from the thighs down. That day changed my life forever. Along with the loss of mobility, I was left with tremendous nervous system pain—pain that most people could never imagine. Imagine having contractions in frequent intervals, like deep throbs, paired with sensations that feel like electrical shocks firing through your body 25 to 30 times an hour. Now imagine that happening every single hour of every single day—for more than two decades. This has been my reality for the past 22 years.

See, in life, *pain is inevitable*. We don't get to choose whether or not we face hardship. But we *do* get to choose how we respond. You will never fulfill your purpose unless you learn how to persevere through the tough times. One thing that helped me was something my old coach taught me when I was a linebacker back in the 1990s. It's a quote I've held onto tightly: **"Tough times do not last long. Tough people do!"**

That mindset became my lifeline.

Fortunately, even after my accident, life wasn't over—it was just different. I met my wife after the accident. She didn't see my wheelchair first—she saw my spirit. With her support and my own determination, I earned my degree in Health with an emphasis in Physical Education and Recreation. I didn't stop there. I became a coach. I had the honor of working with student-athletes at Jackson State University, where I coached college football and led strength and conditioning for the girls' basketball, softball, and volleyball teams for four years. Eventually, I became a high school football coach, too.

And I did it all from a wheelchair.

I wasn't limited by my chair—I was fueled by my purpose. Sports didn't leave me behind. They just opened a new lane for me. I went on to win wheelchair basketball championships, and I had the privilege of representing our country by playing for the USA Wheelchair Softball Team in Tokyo, Japan. I helped lead that team to two back-to-back World Championships. The journey wasn't easy. The pain never stopped. But I became intentional about persevering through it all.

ANTONIO VAN'KEITH WRIGHT

Are you in a difficult situation? What can you do to persevere?

Chapter 10

Perspective

As a person in a wheelchair, I have learned how to adapt and see things from multiple viewpoints. Life looks different when you're not standing in the same position as everyone else—literally and figuratively. For example, my house is still my house, but now that I am in a wheelchair, it's somewhat different. My bathroom is still my bathroom, but now my bathroom and my wheelchair don't mix so easily. What was once convenient and automatic has become something that requires planning, patience, and effort.

See, when I was a five-foot-eleven linebacker, I never even noticed a six-inch sidewalk curb. I could hop up or down one without thinking twice. But now, from the seat of my wheelchair, a six-inch curb is a long way up—and an even longer way down. What used to be invisible is now a daily challenge. I use this example to emphasize a simple but powerful truth: **perspective is important.**

The problem with many people who get into arguments or disagreements is that they believe they are completely right—and that the other person is completely wrong. That kind of perspective is limited and often damaging. When you're stuck thinking only your side is valid, you start believing you're smarter, more informed, or just flat-out better than the other person. But the reality is, you're only looking at one side of a two-sided coin.

I can look at a coin and tell you with full confidence, "It has a heads side." And you could look at the same coin and say, "No, it has a tails side." In that moment, we might both think the other is wrong—but in truth, we're both right. We're just seeing different sides. That's where growth happens—when we realize that **perspective matters**.

We should be intentional about remembering that everyone sees things through a different lens. We all come from different experiences, different upbringings, and different environments. And those experiences shape how we view the world. Each perspective should be valued, even if we don't agree with it. Being open to respectful dialogue allows us to grow. If you tell me about the tails side of the coin and I've only ever known the heads side, then now I have a fuller understanding—of both sides.

Perspective doesn't mean abandoning your truth. It just means acknowledging that your truth is not the only truth.

So, the next time you're in an argument or debate and feel the urge to prove your point beyond all doubt, try to stop yourself for about 10

THE WRIGHT WORKBOOK

seconds. Breathe. Listen. And remember this: **perspective is important.**

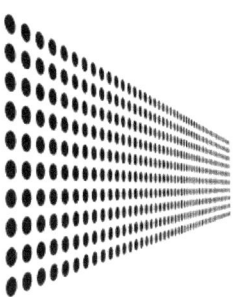

Why is it important to understand someone else's perspective?

_____
_____
_____
_____
_____
_____
_____
_____
_____
_____
_____
_____
_____
_____
_____
_____

Chapter 11
Responsibility

My mother hated to see dishes in the sink. She would always say, "If you use it, wash it. If you see someone else's dishes in the sink, then you wash them, too." Back then, I didn't really understand what my mother was trying to teach me. I just thought she wanted the kitchen to stay clean. But now, I understand it was about much more than just dishes.

Let's say you ate from a plate on Monday and put that unwashed dish in the sink. Then you repeated the process on Tuesday, Wednesday, and for the remainder of the week. What happens? You'd be putting your responsibility to the side. Now, here's the bigger question—who do you expect to fix your problem that you allowed to pile up? See, every choice we make has a consequence, whether it's big or small. Even a ten-year-old can wash his own cereal bowl when he finishes eating. The lesson is simple: **handle your own responsibilities**.

The truth is most of us want our responsibilities to disappear into thin air. We hope that if we ignore them long enough, someone else will step in and handle them for us. But life doesn't work that way. If you don't take care of your responsibilities, they won't go away—they will only pile up. And when they do, the cleanup is much harder than it would have been if you had handled them one dish, one decision, one responsibility at a time.

When you do finally take the time to clean up your bad choices, there is one very important question to ask yourself: **"Did I learn from this mistake, or am I going to repeat it all over again?"** Growth comes when you break the cycle, not when you keep scrubbing the same old plate again and again because you refused to change your habits.

My mother's lesson was bigger than dishes. It was about life. Handle your business. Take care of what is yours. Be accountable for your actions. Because the longer you ignore your responsibilities, the heavier they become.

Responsibility, like those dishes, is yours to manage. The sooner you take care of it, the lighter your load will be.

What responsibilities are you avoiding?

What plan will you create to take care of these responsibilities?

Chapter 12

Conflict

If you are the subordinate and your superior tells you to comply with their request, it is wise to do so. I was taught by my mother at a young age not only to do what I was told but to do it politely and as efficiently as possible. It was a lesson in respect and discipline. Later in life, my wife taught me another important lesson: document everything. Too many times, we let our emotions get in the way of this simple act of self-protection and accountability. But the truth is this—if you are the subordinate, then you are not the one in control. Your true power lies in your effort, in your discipline, and in your honor.

Let's just say that *the conflict* is with your mom or your teacher. It could be with your principal or even with the police. I don't care if it is your boss, a supervisor, or whoever the superior might be—if you are the subordinate, the wisest course of action is to do what is asked of you politely and efficiently. It doesn't mean you agree. It doesn't mean you give up your voice. It simply means you understand the value of handling the moment with wisdom. If the superior is wrong—and sometimes they will be—remember that every boss has a boss. Everyone is accountable to someone.

In the meantime, document everything. Write down what you were assigned, whether it is a project, a task, or any other orders or demands. Keep a record—not to be petty, but to protect your integrity. Documentation allows you to speak with clarity and truth when it matters most.

Understand this clearly—a subordinate acting irrationally, loudly, and belligerently in school might get suspended. A subordinate acting irrationally, loudly, and belligerently with a policeman—especially a young Black man—can get physically harmed, or worse. We live in a world where perception can become reality very quickly. No matter how right you feel you are, never forget the weight of the moment.

Your job is not to escalate the situation but to navigate it with wisdom. Allow the superior to give you, as the subordinate, instructions. Then do your assignment politely and efficiently—no matter how uncomfortable or unfair the situation might feel. That is not weakness; it is strength. It is understanding that self-control is more powerful than raw emotion.

And when the moment has passed, if necessary, take your documentation and seek justice through the proper channels. But in the moment, choose wisdom. Protect your peace. Protect your future.

THE WRIGHT WORKBOOK

How can you handle conflicts with your superiors politely and efficiently?

_____
_____
_____
_____
_____
_____
_____
_____
_____
_____
_____
_____
_____
_____
_____
_____
_____
_____
_____

Chapter 13
Critical Thinking

A person who wants victory in their endeavors must understand what critical thinking is and how to apply it to the circumstances that occur in everyday life. I believe that using critical thinking skills is essential in reaching our goals and overcoming our challenges. *Critical thinking* involves being able to solve a problem and examine information from several different perspectives. To objectively analyze facts and pass judgment, you must understand that critical thinking is self-directed, self-disciplined, self-monitored, and self-corrective thinking. It requires you to step outside of your emotions and personal biases so you can clearly assess a situation and make the best decision possible.

When I was in elementary school, I loved math. Numbers made sense to me. But when I ran into Algebra, everything changed. I began to hate math. I could not understand how X could ever equal a number.

THE WRIGHT WORKBOOK

It just didn't click. For the longest time, I stared at those equations, feeling frustrated and defeated. Then one day, I learned that there is a formula needed to arrive at the answer. Once I understood that simple fact and applied it, Algebra became so much easier for me. I realized that the problem had always been solvable—I just needed the right way to think about it.

That experience taught me a valuable lesson about life. Life is complicated. Sometimes, it feels like one big equation filled with unknowns. But a person who applies critical thinking to their challenges can simplify their problems and be successful at finding the answer. You may not have all the pieces at first, but with patience and a disciplined mind, you can break any problem down and work your way through it.

Critical thinking is not about knowing everything. It's about knowing *how* to think. It's about learning how to ask the right questions, how to seek out reliable information, how to analyze situations from different angles, and how to adjust your thinking when new information comes to light. The more you practice this, the more powerful and effective you become in every area of life.

So, remember—when challenges arise, don't just react. Think. Analyze. Apply wisdom. Because victory belongs to those who are willing to think critically and act accordingly.

ANTONIO VAN'KEITH WRIGHT

Think of a challenge you are facing now. What are the facts?

_____
_____
_____
_____
_____
_____
_____
_____

What choices do you have?

_____
_____
_____
_____
_____
_____
_____
_____

THE WRIGHT WORKBOOK

What is good and bad about each choice?

Chapter 14
Prayer

I don't talk to my God like they talked to God in the Bible. I don't talk to my God the way they talk to God at church. I guess that's because my conversation with Him is a little more *personal*. I talk to Him about *everything*. I pray at night before I sleep, in the morning when I wake, and before I eat every meal. But it doesn't stop there. I also pray when I lose my keys or my phone, when I get mad, sad, or happy, when a car pulls out in front of me, when I am thankful, and even when someone dies. No matter what is going on, I always talk to God.

See, a simple, *"Good morning, Lord! Thank you for letting me see another day!"* would please Him. It doesn't have to be long or formal. It just needs to be from the heart. I often say, "Please guide me through the day and past all evil. Help me to be Your hands of goodness and kindness today." The energy you start with in the morning is important for the entire day. If you begin with a grateful spirit and invite God into your day, you will carry that mindset with you through whatever comes your way.

I don't think you should just pray before you eat and before you go to sleep. You should pray all day, in all kinds of ways! Prayer is not limited to church pews or dinner tables. It is an open line of communication with the One who knows you best and loves you most. Whether it's a whisper, a shout, a song, or a simple thought in the middle of a busy moment—keep that conversation going.

Talk to Him about the big things and the small things. Ask Him for guidance, strength, patience, and peace. Thank Him for the blessings you see and for the ones you don't even realize are happening around you. The more you talk to God, the closer you feel to Him. And the closer you feel to Him, the more you recognize His hand in every part of your life.

So, pray often. Pray honestly. Pray personally. Because God is always listening.

When was the last time your talked to God? What did He say to you?

Chapter 15

Vision

Vision is being able to see your goal completed—even when your goal may seem a little strange to try or a long way off. You must understand that your present situation is often far from where you need to go. My old coach used to say, **"You all are so blinded by the trees that you can't see the forest."** I didn't understand what he was saying at first. But now I see. He was really saying that sometimes we get so stuck on our immediate problems that we can't see the big picture.

I remember the year before we won our junior college state football championship. We had just been beaten by our rivals, and they were celebrating—partying right on our field, in front of us. That moment stung. I sat outside with two of my teammates and watched them. We were disappointed, but that disappointment quickly turned into determination. Right then and there, we made a promise to ourselves: *next year, we were going to beat that same team—on our field.*

The three of us were driven by our vision. See, vision motivated us to be the first ones in and the last ones out at our 4:00 a.m. practices. Vision motivated us to lift heavier weights, to run faster, and to push harder. Vision motivated us to challenge our other teammates to work harder, too, because we knew that to accomplish our goal, it would take all of us.

It wasn't easy. It was a long year filled with sweat, sacrifice, and setbacks. There were mornings when getting up at 4:00 a.m. felt impossible. There were days when the weight room seemed too heavy and the drills too intense. But our vision kept us going. Our vision reminded us why we were doing it.

With great coaches and motivated teammates, we not only became state champions—we also became bowl champions. What once was just a vision—a promise made under the lights after a painful loss—became a reality.

That experience taught me this: *when you have vision, you have power*. Vision helps you rise above discouragement. Vision helps you stay focused when the grind gets hard. Vision helps you pull others with you toward a shared goal. Without it, you get lost in the trees and miss the forest. But with it, you can move mountains.

So, whatever your goal is—see it first in your mind and heart. Then put in the work to make it real. Because vision is the first step to victory.

THE WRIGHT WORKBOOK

What is your vision for your education? What is your vision for your life?

Chapter 16

Determination

I told you about my championship in college, but what I did not disclose was the fact that I was a walk-on during my very first year. I tried out for my college football team four times before I finally made the team. I was cut three times before they allowed me to put pads on and try out in the pre-season two-a-day practices. Despite that disappointing start, I finished my career by scoring the winning touchdown in the state championship game. To overcome such adversity, it took one thing—**determination**.

At any point during that journey, I could have made an excuse to quit. It would have been easy to justify walking away after being cut once, twice, or even three times. But excuses don't help you achieve your goals or win championships. **Determination does.**

The truth is, today, I am paralyzed. But I still understand that life requires responsibility. If my wife was to call the bill collector and tell them that she cannot pay our bills because her husband is in a wheelchair, it would not suffice. Although the fact that I *am* in a wheelchair is true, that truth does not matter to the bill collector. It is simply an excuse in their eyes—an excuse that still will not fulfill our financial obligations.

That example serves as a reminder that excuses—no matter how valid they may seem—do not produce results. Life will not pause to make room for your excuses. Life demands that you rise above your circumstances.

Rather than spend energy justifying why you can't do something, use that energy to **determine how you can.** Determination moves you forward when excuses want to hold you back. Determination fuels progress when circumstances tempt you to quit.

No matter what your personal challenge is—physical limitations, past failures, financial hardship, or rejection—don't let excuses write your story. Let **determination** do the talking. Because at the end of the day, results—not excuses—are what will move you closer to your goals.

What excuses do you need to replace with determination?

Chapter 17

Reliability

I learned how to truly be *reliable* when I was on my junior college championship football team. If the coach told me to hit anything that came in the B-gap, then no matter what else happened, my team could depend on me to take care of my responsibility first and foremost. I understood that my job came before anything else on the field. I was determined to be there, and they knew they could rely on me.

Amazingly, the guy who was a walk-on—and who was one of the slowest guys on the team—ended up catching a blocked field goal late in the fourth quarter and running it back 76 yards to WIN THE STATE CHAMPIONSHIP GAME! That moment taught me something even bigger than the thrill of the win. It taught me that when you are reliable, opportunities will find you—even when others doubt you.

Effective teamwork can only be achieved with reliable team members. We were created to work together. In every phase of life, you will be teaming up with someone. At home, you have your family—that is a team. At school, you have your classmates and your teacher—that is a team. At work, you and your coworkers are a team. No matter where you go or what you do, you are always part of some kind of team.

I learned that just because you have great players on a team, it does not guarantee that those great players will work together to form a great team. That is where **reliability** becomes so important.

Ask yourself this: Are you reliable in doing your job every time, with maximum effort? Can your team rely on you to do your part—whether it is on the field, in the classroom, in the home, or in your career? Reliability is not about being the biggest or the strongest or the fastest. It is about being consistent, committed, and dependable.

I was not the biggest of my teammates. I was not the strongest of my teammates. But I was a teammate who was **reliable**—and that made all the difference. Because when everyone on a team knows they can count on each other, that is when ordinary players accomplish extraordinary things.

THE WRIGHT WORKBOOK

Are you a reliable person? Do you do what you say you will do?

Chapter 18

Forgive

I lost my brother to violence. That kind of pain runs deep and leaves scars that do not fade easily. Some years later, I saw one of the guys who helped cover up that crime. He was walking into a funeral service, struggling to tie his tie. Before I even realized what I was doing, I rolled up on him, helped tie his tie, and whispered these words in his ear, **"I forgive you."**

That moment wasn't about him. It was about freeing myself. Holding onto hate would have only kept me in bondage. This world already has more than enough hate—and it continues to grow every day. However, through my experience, I charge you to demonstrate love and forgiveness in your own lives—and not just when it's convenient or easy. *True forgiveness* is tested when it costs you something.

My father was never there for me or my brother. Growing up without his presence was painful. I carried that wound for years.

However, after I turned 40 years old, his new wife reached out to me, wanting us to reconnect. I wrestled with that decision. But after prayer and reflection, I chose forgiveness. Today, we have a relationship because I told him, face to face, that I loved him and had forgiven him.

Let me be really clear about something: the Bible doesn't read **"like your neighbor as you like yourself"** or **"like your wife as Jesus likes the church"** or **"like your enemies."** No—it says to **love them.** There is a difference between liking and loving. Liking is about *feelings*; loving is about *a choice*.

As I took heed to the good book, I refused to let bitterness and unforgiveness plague my life. Carrying bitterness would have only poisoned my future. Forgiveness released me from that prison.

Forgiveness doesn't excuse what happened. It doesn't erase the pain or suggest that what was done was right. But it frees you to move forward in peace. Life is too short to stay shackled to yesterday's wounds.

So today, I encourage you: choose love. Choose forgiveness. Not because others deserve it, but because ***you*** deserve peace.

Who has done wrong to you? Are you willing to forgive them today?

Chapter 19

Relentless

As a student, reading and spelling did not come easy for me. I had to write notes, rewrite those notes, and then rewrite them again—just to make a B on an exam. It was frustrating at times, but I kept pushing forward. The same young man who could barely read by the fourth grade persevered and eventually graduated from high school with honors, graduated college with honors, is an author of multiple books, mentors youth, and is now the owner of a nonprofit organization that helps wheelchair users compete in adaptive sports.

Having an attitude of relentlessness translates into victory in any phase of life. Too many times, we give up because things get too uncomfortable or too difficult. The moment the path gets rocky, we start to question whether the goal is worth it. But that is exactly when you need to push harder, not quit.

Because of this, we must change the way we think. We must also change the way we respond to difficult times. Quitting cannot be your default response to adversity. We cannot continue to do what has not worked and expect things to be different. If the old mindset hasn't led you to victory, it is time to adopt a new one—**a mindset of relentlessness.**

We cannot allow circumstances to dictate our choices. Circumstances will change. Life will throw unexpected challenges your way. But your choices must remain rooted in a relentless desire to complete your goal. You must decide that no matter how many obstacles appear, you will not be shaken.

You can win—even when you keep losing—by never, ever quitting or giving up. Every failure can be a stepping stone if you keep moving forward. Every setback can be a lesson that fuels your next attempt. Success is not about perfection. It is about persistence.

I am living proof of this. I wasn't the fastest learner, the best speller, or the strongest reader. But I was relentless. And that attitude made all the difference.

So whatever your goal is—keep going. Keep fighting. Keep believing. Because relentlessness will take you further than talent alone ever could.

THE WRIGHT WORKBOOK

What one thing do you want to be relentless about?

Chapter 20

Resilient

When I first became paralyzed in the 1990s, I met my Godfather, Willie L. Harvey, who introduced me to adaptive sports. My first sport was wheelchair basketball. Willie was a disabled Vietnam vet who had been paralyzed since the 1970s. He used to stand 6'6" tall, and he carried a wealth of wisdom and experience.

Back in the 90s, sports chairs didn't come with bars to stop you from flipping over backward. Willie would generously lend his chairs out to youngsters like me who were just starting out. My only problem was that his chair was too tall and set up too high for me. This meant the chair was very top-heavy and tippy, which made it a real challenge to control.

Willie kept count of all my falls. I flipped over backward and forward more than a hundred times. I even flipped backward at the free throw line while sitting completely still. The flipping didn't stop—not even during the national championship tournament. Every time I flipped, the crowd would hush at first, unsure of what to expect. But Willie? He would laugh so hard and make a funny remark to get everyone laughing. An able-bodied man or two would usually run over to help me up.

I hit that hard wood floor over and over again. It would have been easy to give up. But that did not stop me from becoming **Tournament Rookie of the Year**. It didn't stop me from helping my new team win the second of our four national wheelchair basketball championships.

Everyone on the court, in the stands, and on my team knew one thing—I was about to do my job. Regardless of my shortcomings, regardless of how many times I hit the floor, I was going to continue attacking with intensity, focus, and heart.

Nelson Mandela once said, **"Do not judge me by my success, judge me by how many times I fell down and got back up again."** I lived that truth on the hardwood floor and in life.

So, my message to you is this: **be resilient**. Life will knock you down. You will fall. But what matters is that you get back up—every single time. Because it's not about how many times you fall. It's about how many times you rise.

What do you need to try again?

THE WRIGHT WORKBOOK

About the Author

Antonio Vankeith Wright is affectionately known as Coach Wright to those he coached at Jackson State University, several high schools in Mississippi, and now around the world. Antonio is the CEO and founder of Metro Area Community Empowerment, Inc., a nonprofit organization dedicated to championing capabilities and providing opportunities for at-risk youth and individuals with physical disabilities.

His first book, *From a Label to a Brand*, is an autobiography. In it, he shares how he dealt with many facets of life, such as the divorce of his parents, living in a single-parent, low-income household, gang activity, low academic achievement, and behavioral and emotional problems. He also chronicles the death of his brother and the motor vehicle accident that left him paralyzed from the waist down.

Coach Wright's faith and tenacious spirit have helped him overcome life's obstacles and live a life of joy. His reality allowed him to turn his pain into his passion. His goal is simple yet profound: to be an infection that refuses to be infected.